HIGH Tech

vs

The HIGHEST Tech

by Jeff Tichelar

Milk & Honey Ministries
5500 E. 45th St N
Bel Aire, KS 67220

Library of Congress Control Number: 2019939265

The proceeds from the sale of this book go toward missions projects.

Clayton and Shirley Tichelar
50th Wedding Anniversary (2005)

Clayton Wayne Tichelar 9/14/1931 - 8/4/2016
Shirley Joan Tichelar 1/7/1932 - 8/27/2008

In remembrance of Mom & Dad…

You taught your children (those you gave birth to and those God put in your arms) by your words and actions how to work, live, love and succeed in finding peace and joy in life. Part of your powerful example was your open and humble spirit that enabled both of you to receive Jesus as your Lord and Savior later in life.

We can now look forward to our grand reunion one day because we have each put our faith and trust in Jesus as our Creator and Savior. Thank you for all the lives you touched and blessed!

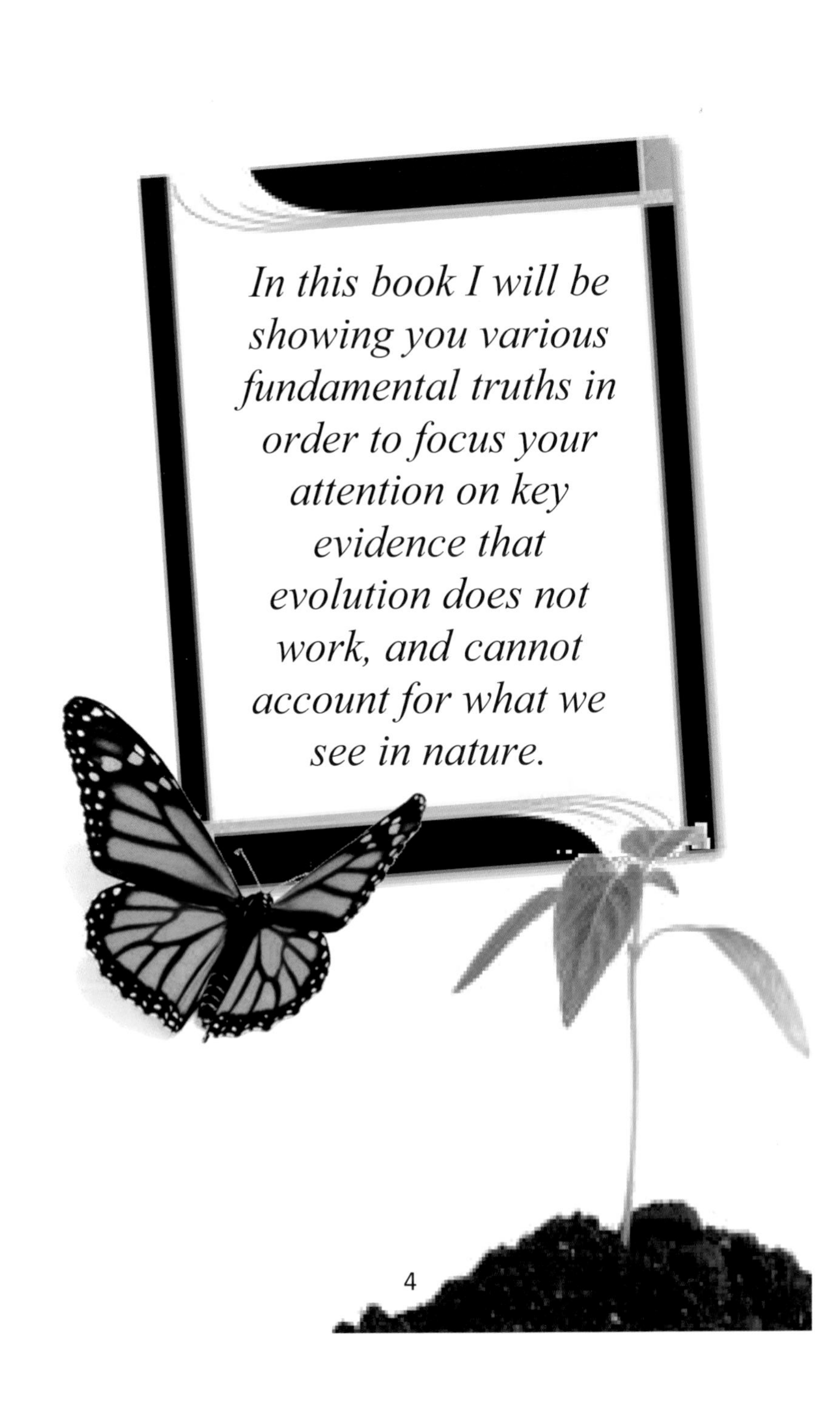

In this book I will be showing you various fundamental truths in order to focus your attention on key evidence that evolution does not work, and cannot account for what we see in nature.

Table of Contents

Introduction

Charles Darwin, a famous prophet & promoter of the "religion of evolution," (and make no mistake: it is a religion) said, ***"The mystery of the beginning of all things is insoluble by us; and I for one must be content to remain an agnostic."*** In order to qualify as a scientific fact, a theory must be observable or reproducible. Creation and evolution fail on both accounts, therefore both theories are a matter of faith!

Charles Darwin was not an atheist! He admitted that he was not sure of his own theory. He also went on to say something VERY IMPORTANT! ***"If it could be demonstrated that any COMPLEX ORGAN existed which could not possibly have been formed by numerous, successive slight modifications, my theory would absolutely break down."***

The design and function showcased in nature has helped me acknowledge the existence of a powerful and awesome Creator. This is my personal choice. My purpose is not to undermine your freedom of choice, but to provide facts and information to consider.

The purpose of this book is to clearly and scientifically demonstrate from nature that evolution does not support the gradual development of any life forms – complex or simple!

My desire is that we will all have the benefit of nature's witness in drawing a conclusion about our origin.

Why Read This Book?

A Note from the Author

With so many wonderful books available on the subjects of nature, origins and apologetics – do we need another book in this space? You tell me. Here is what I have strived to accomplish with this book. First, the book is written for young, old and professional readers alike. Complicated and/or scientific information is written in a style and at a level younger readers can understand and enjoy, while older and more informed readers will also be challenged and gain insight into complex bio-designs and function. **This book is exciting – a page-turner** (no fillers)! Every word, every sentence is necessary and contributes to understanding the subject at hand. **Every reader will learn something new and many will have their minds challenged as they ponder the facts presented!**

Please note that in an effort to be efficient with extra space at the end of chapters, I have chosen to include personal pictures of my family and ministry to help establish rapport with my readers. Since these pictures are not part of the message, I hope they will not confuse or distract you from that message.

May the reader be blessed,

Jeff Tichel

A few fundamental truths as we consider our origin and the theory of evolution.

1) If evolution were true, we should expect that in nature, animals would be more similar than they are different! Not the vast array, variety and unusual rarities we see - a spectacular variety of life forms or kinds (species) that are all fully functional, complex and reproduce their own kind.

2) There are NO examples of anything evolving into anything else! There are NO transitional forms in the fossil record, though there have been several attempts to mischaracterize some discoveries, and claim a transition. They always prove to be a hoax, fraud or fabrication. There is no evidence for Darwinian Evolution, as in one kind turning into a different kind! None!

3) Genetic adaptations, also known as horizontal variations, are not evolution as in one species changing into a different species. Climate, diet, environment and

breeders have produced over 200 varieties of dogs – long hair, short hair, different temperaments, 4 lb. Chihuahuas and 180 lb. Great Danes – but dogs remain dogs! Adaptations are a function of Intelligent Design that help all life forms survive changing conditions, but those changes are limited by boundaries set within DNA.

> "Not one change of species into another is on record… we cannot prove that a single species has been changed." - Charles Darwin, My Life and Letters, Vol. 1, p. 210

4) Evolution offers no reasonable explanation for the source of **life and intelligence**.

5) Evolution has no answer to the problem of "irreducible complexity," that requires complex organs to exist fully functional for life forms to exist and live… Heart, lungs, brain, eyes, ears, immune system, etc.

Helpful Definitions:

1. **Intelligent Design** - the theory that life, or the universe, cannot have arisen by chance and was designed and created by an intelligent entity.
2. **Irreducible complexity** - a fancy phrase that means a single system which is composed of several interacting parts, and where the removal of any one of the parts makes the existence and function of the system impossible.

I want the readers of this book to clearly see the great divide between the high tech designs of mankind, and the Highest Tech designs that are far above and beyond our capabilities and therefore point to One greater than us.

The House Fly

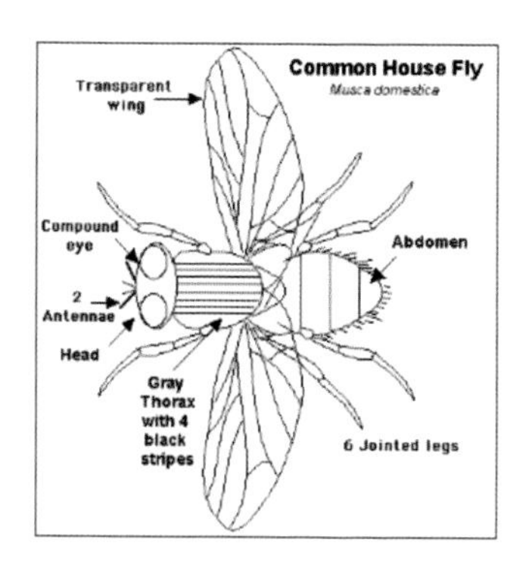

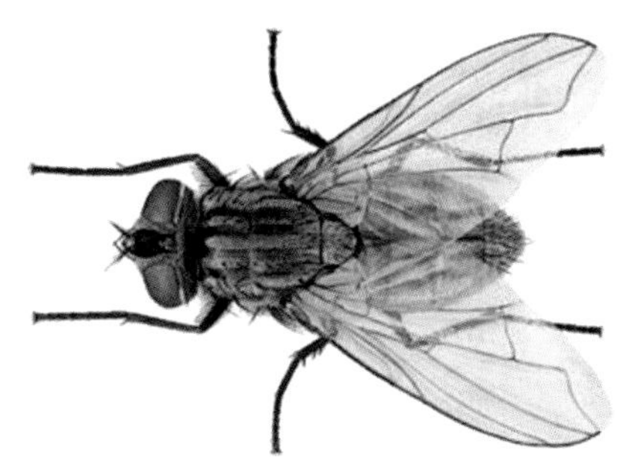

I will begin our study of the Highest Tech with the small, modest House Fly. The House Fly is an insect made up of head, thorax, and abdomen. The thorax is what I want to focus on. It is the main platform of the fly's Highest Tech design.

Special hinges mount the fly's wings to the thorax. Those hinges and much of the thorax are made from the same material called Resilin. Resilin is a million times more efficient than a rubber band in both strength and function. Rubber bands degrade, loose their resilience and are vulnerable to every sort of environmental condition, such as cold, heat, ultra violet rays, chemicals, etc. Rubber bands also break!

Scientists have concluded that Resilin is as near a perfect protein rubber as they have ever seen or imagined. There is no man-made rubber or elastic material that even comes close. The fly's incredible wing cycles (200 to 300 cycles per second) would not be possible without it.

Here's how it works. The brain sends an electrical message to the wing muscles to activate them up and down. The start uses the most effort, just like starting up an engine.

The sudden burst of electric signal to the wings causes them to go up.

The muscle stretches the thorax, making it longer and thinner while storing energy. When the wing reaches its maximum designed height, the brain cancels the electrical signal causing the wings to rebound. With the rebound power, another muscle has just turned on. The thorax quickly becomes shorter and thicker. Because it is thicker, it stretches the Resilin sideways, pulling the wings down. Stored energy causes the wings to snap up to the high position again.

The pulsing wings require exact, timed, electric signals from the brain to the muscles. And all this is in a fraction of a second! Remember at least 200 signals per second to fly. Just think about this… two hundred times per second the thorax must change its shape and rebound. However, the muscles do not have to work very hard because of the Resilin.

One of the most amazing proteins known to man is Resilin, but man did not make it!

And man cannot duplicate it! Man has high tech, but nature reveals the Highest Tech!

I would like to briefly look at one more of the countless design features of the fly that add to its resumé of "Highest Tech" equipment.

The fly is at the top of the food chain when it comes to insect-scavengers, but they do have many enemies looking for a slice of tasty house fly! (Spiders, frogs, lizards, some birds and wasps.)

In addition to its incredible speed and maneuverability, thanks in great part to Resilin, the fly has awesome eyes.

Notice the Highest Tech design of the fly's compound eyes.

Picture how hard it would be for one man to keep track of all the activity in a casino; watching for cheating at gaming tables, stealing, vandalizing, drunken behaviors, etc. He would need dozens, maybe hundreds of close circuit TVs to keep watch, but how many could one man monitor? You would need a large room full of monitors and a small army of people to watch them!

The fly has between 3,000 and 6,000 simple eyes in each bulbous eye globe which make up the compound eyes. Unlike eyes that focus on specific targets, the fly has a mosaic view of everything – right, left, front, up, down - all at once! It is like having thousands of monitors to view and process every second.

If that were not enough eyes, they also have an additional 3 simple eyes called OCELLI located between the two compound eyes. They are part of its navigational equipment/compass so the fly always knows which way is up. This is so incredible; I hope you can see the awesome Highest Tech design of the fly's compound eyes!

East-African Termites

In nature, there are many awesome examples of incredible architecture and design. (Beavers, birds, bees, etc.)

It's funny that God would cause one of the smallest creatures on earth, seemingly handicapped by blindness, to build and maintain some of the largest and most elaborate animal homes on earth.

The East-African termite can build the equivalent of super skyscrapers, fully air-conditioned in some of the hottest locations on earth. They are also complete with internal food supplies and subway systems (tunnels). One well dug by these termites was found to be 125 feet deep in order to reach water.

Many termite colonies number in the millions of tenants. The structures they build are made from small bits of soil cemented together with their own saliva, yet the outer shell is as hard as concrete. Some termite mounds that are still standing, are over one hundred years old.

It is a wonder of God that He has created a tiny, blind creature that builds a skyscraper over twenty feet tall! If scaled to man's size, it would be over 1,000 feet with no special construction equipment or tools. God provided them everything needed at birth.

The structures include a complex ventilation system complete with ducts and chambers designed to filter the air through porous walls and allow stale air to escape. This reveals the special knowledge God has written in their DNA. Remember, they are born with all the knowledge necessary. No one is needed to teach them what to do. Man must account for the source of this intelligence, and functional design.

I cannot credit lifeless chemicals with the ability to produce this wonder!

Spider Silk

From the food the spider eats, its little, internal, chemical laboratory and production factory produces a liquid that turns to silk when it hits the air! If you think this was produced by evolution… a purely natural explanation without intelligence or design, then answer this, "Can the most state of the art science laboratory on earth produce a liquid that can be put into a squeezable ketchup bottle and has all the properties of spider silk?"

Here are the properties to match…

1. When the liquid is excreted and pulled from one of the spider's spinnerets, it almost instantly turns into a solid strand. That strand is 5 times stronger than steel, yet lighter and more flexible.
2. The spider does not just produce one kind of silk. That would be fantastic enough, but spiders produce seven unique types of silk.

3. The silk has 4 different properties: stiff, flexible, sticky and non-sticky depending on the spiders needs.
4. There are 3 types of glue coating: Temporary, permanent and a blend.
5. The special purposes of Spider Silk include: draglines, cocoons, traps for prey, food storage and some silk that is so thin that it is nearly invisible.

One individual spider does not have all seven types of silk, but at least three types if a male and four types if a female (additional egg sack silk). The spider's production factories are so efficient that one average meadow of approximately two million spiders per acre can produce enough silk to reach the moon. For conservation, when finished, the spider will eat the silk.

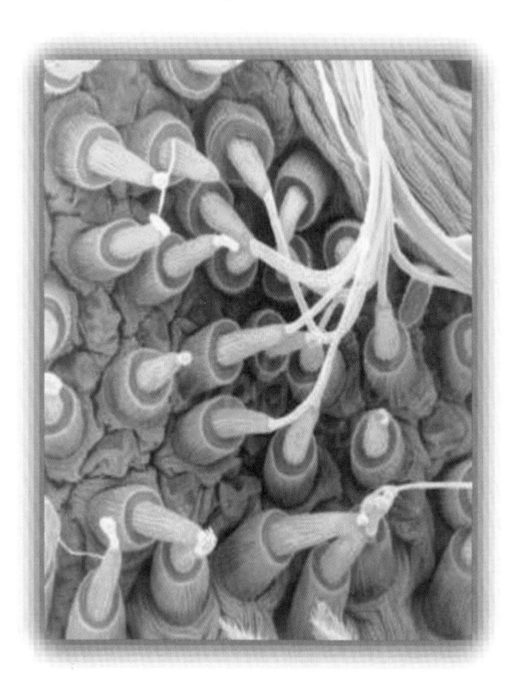

The silk is so light in weight that enough silk thread to stretch around our planet would weigh only ¾ of a pound. Quoting from an American Science News magazine, "On a human scale, a web resembling a fishing net could catch and stop a passenger plane." One cord, that is as thick as a pencil could stop a 747 jet!"

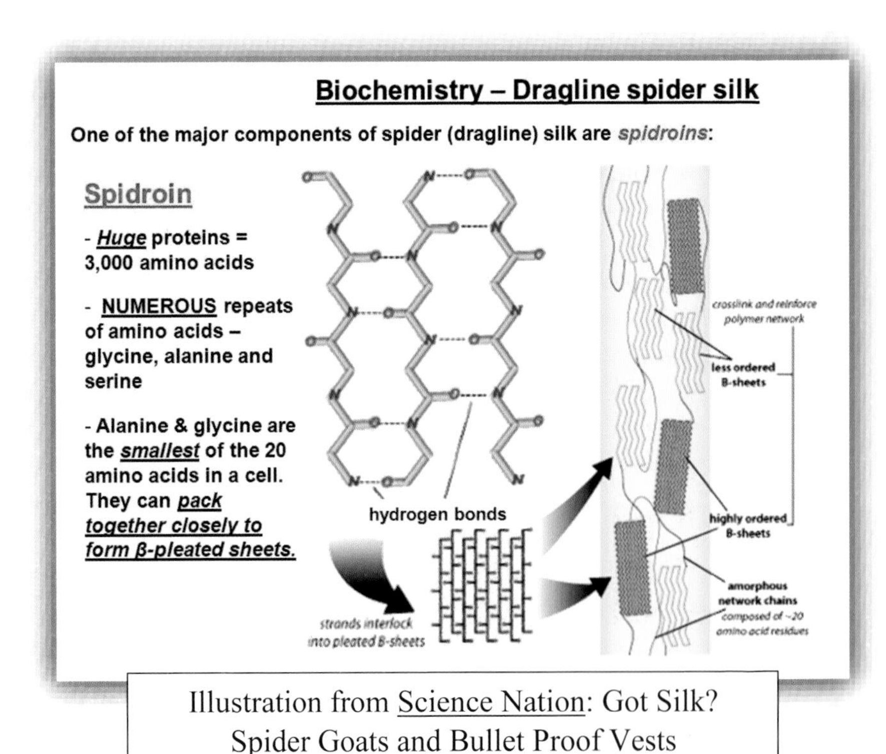

Illustration from Science Nation: Got Silk? Spider Goats and Bullet Proof Vests

One researcher from Curie Journal, April 2010 Vol 3, commented, “How can the thread spun by such a tiny creature have properties vastly superior to rubber and steel, the products of centuries of accumulated human knowledge?”

Another article imagined, “Once the spider’s chemical miracle can be replicated fully, then a great many useful materials could be produced, such as safety belts, surgical sutures that leave no scar and bullet-proof fabric that is light and comfortable.”(Biometrics: Technology Imitates Nature)

When I learned about the properties of Spider Silk, I could not deny the existence of the Highest Tech!

Electrical Eels

There is a fish four feet long and five to six inches in diameter that can generate an electric current more powerful than the electric current generated by your car's charging system!

One experiment revealed that a 3 foot eel could produce a maximum current of 450 to 600 volts. Your household current is 110-120 volts. A standard light bulb uses 60 watts of power. The electric eel at 600 volts and 1000 watts generates enough electricity to light a small house. The discharge is enough to knock down and kill a full grown horse. **BUT HOW?**

The electricity is generated in special glands that are located behind the head and extend along the length of the body. The skin and those glands serve as conductors for the electricity.

Now since this eel's home is in the warm waters of the Amazon and Orinoco rivers of South America, our Lord knew that this fish that looks like a big meat sausage, living in a neighborhood infested with savage piranhas would need a little help ☺.

The electric eel is able to self-generate an electrical field (fence) around itself for protection, and also to stun its own food. **An electric generator from evolution?** Evolutionists reject intelligent design while insisting that given enough time; evolution will produce every example of spectacular design displayed in nature. Personally, I have chosen to put my trust in an Intelligent Designer, not long periods of time.

Golf Balls and Sugar Beet Pollen

What do a golf ball and sugar beet pollen have in common?

The golf ball has 392 dimples. Once, golf balls were smooth, but by accident it was discovered that balls with dimples (old, beat up balls) traveled up to 4 times farther than smooth ones. You see, without the dimples, the air that touches the surface of the smooth ball would not move. Without air movement, there is friction. And where there is friction, things do not move as fast and as far. There is a thin layer of air that wants to stick to the surface of the smooth ball. The 392 dimples act like little fans and blow away the air that wants to stick to the surface. They fan away the friction.

GOD did not design the golf ball, but He did design the scientific law that man discovered by accident. And the proof that God understood this scientific law first is Sugar Beet pollen.

The pollen of a Sugar Beet looks exactly like a golf ball - but on a much smaller scale. You need a microscope to see the wondrous awesome design of God at this size and scale. For the same reason man puts dimples on golf balls, God designed Sugar Beet pollen with dimples so that the pollen would travel farther!

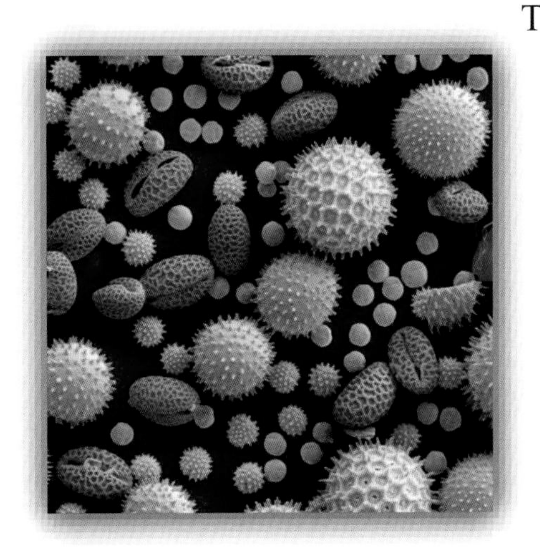

The microscopic Sugar Beet pollen has 60 dimples. The precision and detail of design at this size and scale is truly AWE-INSPIRING! The wind must blow the pollen from one plant to another, or there would be no pollenization. Man discovered the need for dimples on golf balls by accident... but God designed the Sugar Beet pollen with dimples from the beginning on purpose. Please take notice of the INTELLIGENT DESIGN God showcases in creation every day!

Three man team built home for the missionaries in the Amazon Jungle in 2001. Jeff with children from the Satta Maui Tribe.

Rattlesnakes

The rattlesnake, as with most snakes, is an awesome hunter with very sophisticated equipment that defies the theory of evolution. Consider that the rattlesnake has the ability to detect the faintest trace of scent in air molecules and instantly analyze them for identification.

How? God has equipped the rattlesnake with something called the "Jacobson's Organ." As the snake draws its tongue into its mouth, it rubs the tip of his tongue against a special organ in the roof of his mouth (very small and compact). Instantly, the Jacobson's Organ does a chemical analysis and is able to identify friend, foe, meal, etc. with 100% accuracy. Contrast this with the "efficiency" of any C.S.I. laboratory across the country!

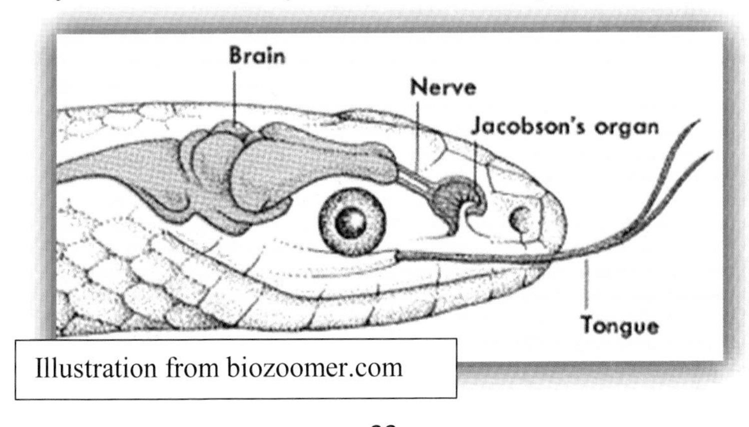

Illustration from biozoomer.com

When a crime is discovered, a person or team must go to the scene of the crime and spend hours gathering potential evidence on swabs and in test tubes. After this, the evidence is driven to a massive criminal science laboratory with millions of dollars' worth of special equipment, computers and a small army of employees to hopefully, days later, come up with evidence of who was there to commit the crime.

If the Jacobson's Organ is not enough to get you to say WOW, then I will have to tell you about one more of the rattlesnake's Highest Tech designs!

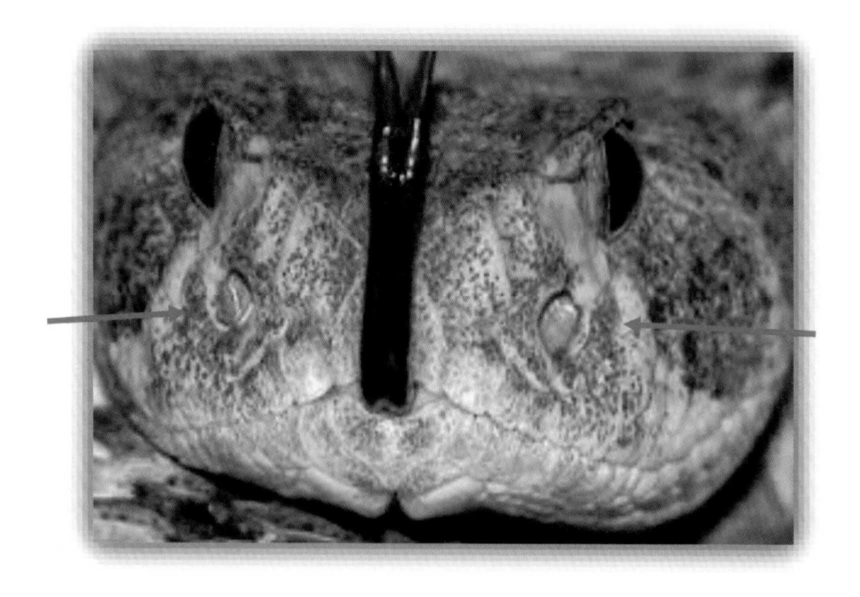

The rattlesnake has two small openings on his face called PITS. The two pits are each filled with 150,000 special temperature sensitive cells. Those 300,000 nerve cells can detect a mouse (in compete darkness) running across his path 300 feet away. **Still not impressed?!**

This temperature detection equipment is so sensitive that the snake can easily pick up the heat signature left by the mouse's foot print several seconds after the mouse has passed! **Question: how much heat do you think a mouse leaves in its footprint?** The rattlesnake is capable of detecting a temperature differential of 1/2,000th of a degree Fahrenheit!

I can only say WOW! I cannot credit natural processes for this complex system.

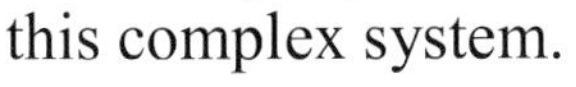

Jeff in the Amazon Jungle with the Mission Team. Building four room school house for Marubo Tribe in 2000.

Bombardier Beetles

The little Bombardier Beetle has many enemies that try to make a meal out of him. Our awesome Creator & Designer, who is also a God of variety, decided to make this little guy a "gun slinger."

Remember that there are many forms of protection for different animals. For example, camouflage, poison, spines, teeth, speed, etc. But in this case, the Lord must have thought the kids (adults like me too) would get a kick out of a little beetle the size of a lady bug with a double barrel shotgun.

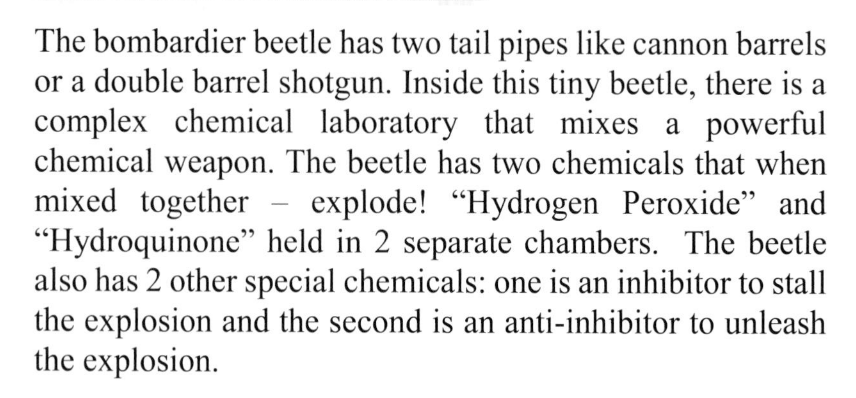

The bombardier beetle has two tail pipes like cannon barrels or a double barrel shotgun. Inside this tiny beetle, there is a complex chemical laboratory that mixes a powerful chemical weapon. The beetle has two chemicals that when mixed together – explode! "Hydrogen Peroxide" and "Hydroquinone" held in 2 separate chambers. The beetle also has 2 other special chemicals: one is an inhibitor to stall the explosion and the second is an anti-inhibitor to unleash the explosion.

When under threat, the little beetle is able, in a fraction of a second, to load the Hydrogen Peroxide and Hydroquinone into the pipes with the inhibitor (so not to blow himself up).

At just the right moment, the fourth chemical which is the anti-inhibitor is added to release the explosive action.

Since the beetle's design includes a fully movable gun barrel controlled by its muscles, the beetle is able to aim the barrels directly behind, or flex 180^0 and fire forward under its belly without losing time trying to turn around. He can also fire off to either side in a 360^0 circle.

This blast is a 212^0 noxious, hot, smelly gas that is delivered in a pulsed fashion of 1000 cycles per second. To the human ear it sounds like one blast, but it is not! A single blast would knock the beetle off its feet; not very efficient for a quick getaway! So our Lord provided a "pulsed" explosion that can be seen with high speed cameras. NASA propulsion engineers are studying this beetle and trying to unravel the mystery of the "PULSED" explosion.

Yes, that's correct. NASA engineers are studying a little creature that God made the size of a ladybug trying to learn its secret. Attributing all this fantastic design to natural processes and lifeless chemicals requires more faith than believing in Intelligent Design.

Discipleship Intern Training Program Class of 1985-86
Jeff with Instructors: William MacDonald, Jean Gibson, Carl Knott and Don Robertson

Jeff with sister, Kim and identical twin brother Craig, nieces Amanda & Meghan and nephew Christian

Geckos

The Gecko is an amazing lizard for many reasons, but one feature stands out to me that is especially awesome - he has GREAT FEET!

The Gecko's ability to walk on virtually any surface including polished glass upside down, presents a real "show and tell" moment. The technological design of this animal goes way beyond the limits of human technology. It is only now with the aid of the electron microscope that we can begin to unveil and understand the amazing structures on the Gecko's feet, but we cannot duplicate what we see! So what is the secret of the Gecko's feet?

I am going to let Dr. Jonathan Sarfati explain this wonder of God in creation, quoting from Creation Magazine…

> "In Creation (Magazine), we reported on how a gecko can stick to almost any surface, so it can even run upside down on a ceiling of polished glass. This is due to the way tiny chemical forces are exploited by tiny hairs called setae, about 1/10 of a millimeter long and packed 5,000 per square millimeter (three million per square inch). The end of each seta has about 400-1,000 branches ending in a spatula like structure about 0.2-0.5 microns-

less than 1/50,000 of an inch long (a micron is 1/1,000 of a millimeter). This is an amazingly fine structure that researchers said was 'beyond the limits of human technology.' But this is not enough - it would do the gecko no good to have this amazing foot if it could only stick - it must also unstick quickly. The gecko manages this with the 'unusually complex behavior' of uncurling its toes when attaching, and unpeeling while detaching."

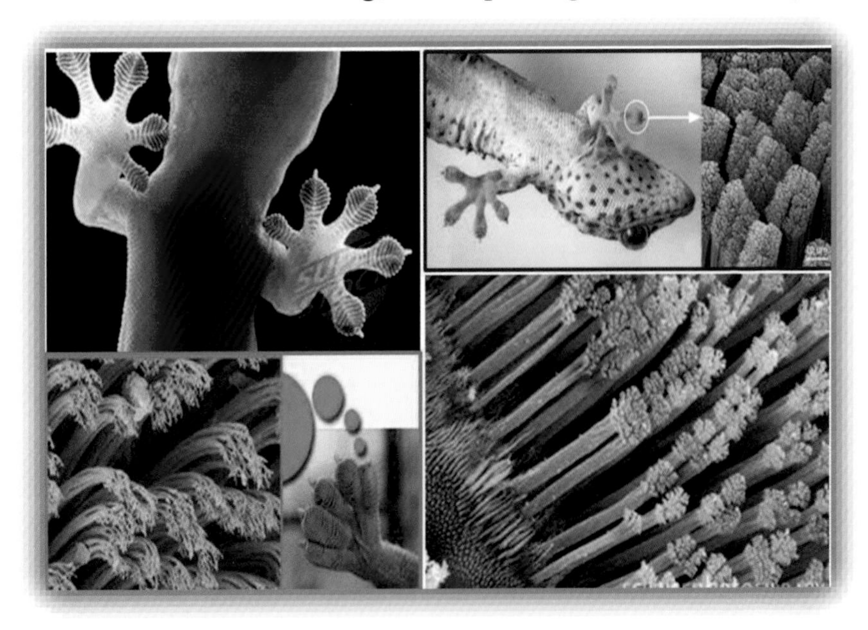

I believe that the level of complexity, demonstrated in this animal's feet, points to Intelligent Design. The laws of Chemistry and Physics are combined to do what looks like magic! This is something that man can only discover, but man cannot duplicate! What an amazing example of the Highest Tech!

"His great works are too marvelous to understand. He performs miracles without number." -Job 9:10 NLT

Dolphins

I want to compare man's soundwave based detection systems (radar/sonar) with the **auditory imaging systems** we find in nature (God's creation). Echolocation is used by mammals like dolphins, whales and bats.

One science paper I read on this subject entitled, Echolocation: Communication of Marine Mammals, Bats and Humans, wrote, "…dolphins produce sound by squeezing air through their nasal passages beneath the blowhole." The melon on the forehead of the dolphin is used to direct the soundwaves ahead of himself. After the soundwaves bounce off the target, they are received through the lower jaw and processed in a special region of the dolphin's brain.

The echolocation of certain dolphins is so acute that experiments show that they can detect with 75% accuracy the difference in the wall thickness of a piece of pipe to 1/100th of an inch (2 pages in this book)! The aquatic version of echolocation is truly fantastic!

Bats

Although dolphins are an amazingly complex and awesome animal with a complex biosonar system, I would like to focus on the bat for our comparison to man's technological abilities.

There are over 1000 species of bats, which accounts for more than 25% of the total number of mammal species. God made bats an important part of the ecosystem and is obviously fond of them – because He made so many! The very small ones are awfully cute!

Bats vary greatly in size, ranging from the very small Bumble Bee and Australian Rain Forest Bats that are the size of a peanut with a 6-inch wing span up to the size of a squirrel with a 6-foot wing span. But regardless of size, all bats use echolocation, including the tiny bats who have a brain the size of a **pencil eraser** or in some cases even smaller!

Bats produce sounds for echolocation that range from biosonar pulses to clicks and other calls. One research scientist wrote, "It's a beautiful, complicated and highly accurate form of prey capture that is thoroughly supported by the bat's innate neural mechanisms." That, my friends, is a HUGE understatement. (Taken from Model Systems in Neuroethology: Echolocation in the Bat)

Before I expand on the details of bat echolocation, let's first consider one area of man's detection and navigation technology.

Man fills a large building with tons and tons of complicated radar equipment and computers to monitor air traffic in order to prevent mid-air collisions between planes. Large cities have hundreds of air traffic control centers manned by thousands of specially trained air traffic controllers. Each controller monitors the flight paths of approximately 8-10 aircraft at a time, watching little green dots and making sure they do not get too close.

Bats fly in and out of dark caves at night. Some of these caves are home to bat colonies of millions of bats. In the case of Bracken Cave in Texas, there is a population of over 20 million bats.

That number of bats can consume **200 tons of insects in one night**! Imagine the ecological impact on man and crops if that one colony of bats did not maintain a balance with the many pesty insects. Bats are the best insect killers on the planet. Little Brown Bats (North American) can catch and eat 1200 mosquitos per hour. **Wow**!

Let's go back to our comparison of man's technology and a bat's echolocation. Remember, one air traffic control center may track hundreds of planes in the sky, but bats are able (millions of bats – thousands at a time!) to fly in and out of a cave opening the size of a 2-car garage with zero collisions and NO mistakes! **Think of it…**bats flying in huge groups, countless objects to avoid, searching for food, etc.

There is a situation people deal with called, *The Cocktail Party Effect*, whereby you try to focus in on and hear one person in a loud party while music is blasting and people are yelling. For the bats flying in groups of hundreds or thousands at a speed of 10 meters per second, and being barraged with echoes from the ground, trees and other objects; this becomes a ***"cocktail party nightmare"*** for the bat!

And still the bat is able to segregate echoes to the point of creating a 3-dimentional picture in his brain in a millisecond. **It is so fantastic!**

Can't you see the Creator's genius?!

The bat, in order to correctly determine distance, must also adjust and compensate for the "Doppler Effect." Sound waves are compressed after impacting their target causing them to return at a higher frequency. This is called Doppler Shift Compensation.

That short millisecond pulse of sonar returns with an **insane** amount of information and that information must be processed unconsciously like when we talk, listen and see without concentration. Remember, the bat is sending out sound waves at a rate of 200 pulses per second and every one of those 200 pulses (per second) is returning with information to process! The bat's auditory imaging system is **sending, receiving and processing hundreds of pieces of spatial, mathematical and abstract information in a fraction of a second.** When flying in groups, the bat may receive over 100,000 echoes (its own mixed with those of other bats in the group) that must be sorted, separated and discriminated in a fraction of a second. The bat can detect and avoid an obstacle the width of a piece of thread in a 3D field of view! The bat can determine size, shape, texture and more.

We know much of this information through the hard work and commitment of countless researchers. Sadly many do not recognize or desire to know our great loving Creator who designed these complex systems. Their efforts nonetheless reveal the complex and Highest Tech work of the Creator.

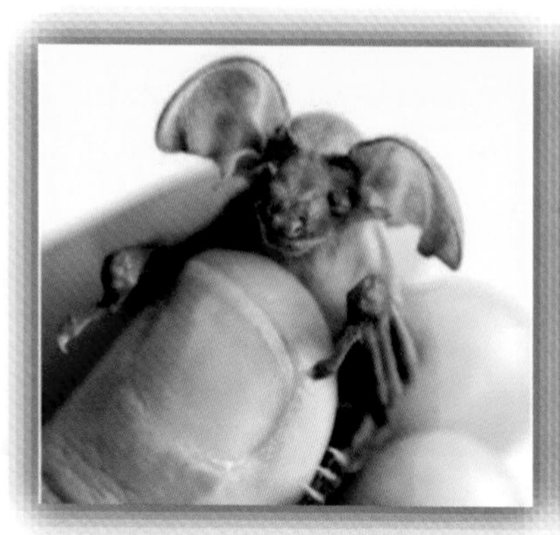

I would like to share a few quotes from these scientists and researchers (in their own words).

> "There are so many pieces of information coded into the pulses and echoes that a bat hears, it is impossible to cover them all in one summary. The following is a list of

cues that the bat can discern from what it hears: relative velocity of a target, flutter of a target, range, size, fine characteristics, azimuth (angular distance to an object) and elevation. This information is encoded in the amplitude of returning echoes, in the delay between echo and pulse, the Doppler shift between pulse and echo and many other combinations of factors. **The bat appears to be an amazing signal processing machine that has an accuracy of 99%!**" (emphasis added)

Quote from "Model Systems in Neuroethology – Echolocation in Bats."

"Some bat senses, like echolocation, are so attuned that researchers are turning to them to inspire technologies in autonomous vehicles, drones, remote submersibles and sonar."

Quote from "Little Bats, Impressive Resumes," Johns Hopkins University's Bat Lab

"Bat species that forage for insects need to be able to actually change their path and change their planning in flight, depending on what's going on with their target," Wu-Jung Lee, a physics researcher at the University of Washington, tells Science Friday. "A bat's echolocation can help enable that change in flight path and that's a capability that our sonar systems currently do NOT have."

Let's get this straight: man with his intelligent design requires hundreds of buildings, full of thousands of technicians, with tons and tons of equipment to monitor the aircraft that fly in our skies. And the bat with all its "air traffic control equipment" in a region of the brain **half the size of a grain of rice** does the same job better and faster with zero mistakes!

"Ears that hear and eyes that see – the Lord has made them both." –Proverbs 20:12 NIV

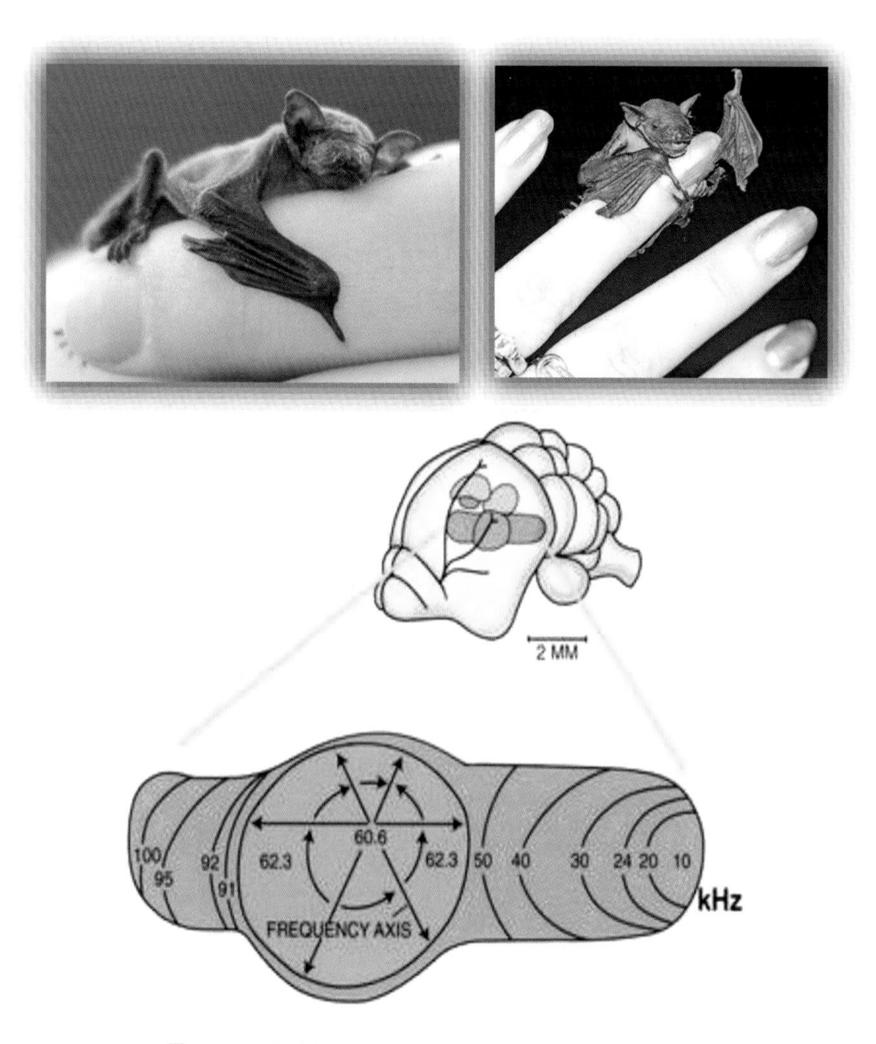

Tonotopic Map in the Bat Auditory Cortex

I am very grateful for the excellent research work (which includes the above illustration) of two people that helped me understand and appreciate the bat.

“What the Bat’s Voice Tells the Bat’s Brain”
Nachum Ulanovsky and Cynthia F. Moss

Whales

The blue whale is the largest animal that has ever lived on earth.

This mammal (not a fish) can grow to be 100 feet in length and weigh an amazing 200 tons, equal to 50 adult bull elephants. This is even larger than the largest dinosaur that ever lived.

Could such a creature evolve? In constructing the evolutionary tree, how in the world does a whale evolve into a butterfly? Or vice versa? As stated previously, there are no examples in the fossil record of any animal evolving into a different animal. Darwin confuses this issue with adaptations like different beaks in birds, colors, etc. There is no change in kind, and no mechanism to add new information to the animal's DNA/blueprint.

Whales breathe air. Females produce milk for their young, just like us. (But we did not evolve from whales!) Blue whales feed in the cold oceans near the North & South poles. They travel to warm tropical seas during the summer to mate.

Here are some incredible facts about Blue Whales:

Their heart weighs an unbelievable half-ton (1,000 lbs.). Their tongues weigh 3 tons (6,000 lbs.). The Blue Whale is huge, but can still reach speeds of over 30 mph. It can leap out of the water and swim on its back. All the result of incredible design!

The blue whale has no teeth. It feeds on plankton (very small plants) and krill (a very tiny shrimp-like creature). Every day, a single blue whale eats 5 tons (10,000 lbs.) of tiny microscopic food. It filters the plankton through a strainer system of thin bony plates in its mouth called the baleen. This fantastic design points me to a fantastic Designer – the Highest Tech!

Think about this for a moment: God designed the largest animal that has ever lived to feed on some of the smallest food sources.

Just imagine the reproduction rates that have to be in place to create the balance we see in the ocean with its fantastic population of creatures. What would happen if ocean life were not in perfect balance?

If one blue whale consumes 10,000 pounds of food per day, multiplied by all the other whales, think of the reproductive "blooms" necessary to feed them. Then think of the reproductive blooms without the massive animals to consume the right amount.

Get this one balance wrong, and it would be impossible to support the life of whales or the entire ocean would become jammed with microscopic food like a clogged pipe; nothing could live. That's just one small example of this balance.

When a blue whale baby is born, it is already 23 feet long and weighs 2000 pounds. The mother feeds the baby with nutritious milk that is as thick as a malt, 40 times a day. The baby grows at a rate of 9 pounds per hour. By its first birthday, the baby weighs 50,000 pounds - more than 10 times the birth weight.

Whales are included in this book because they are a great showcase of God's Highest Tech design. One example is the whale's super sensitive sensing system that rivals our own ultrasound machines.

The book, Whale Nation, describes it so wonderfully:

> *"Their brains are six times the size of Man's... Exchanging information with high resolution, detecting sounds a microsecond long. Unearthly creatures inhabiting a medium 800 times denser than air. The whale moves in a sea of sound. Shrimp snap, plankton seethe, fish croak, gulp, drum their air*

bladders and are scrutinized by echolocation, a light massage of sound touching the skin.

These small-toothed whales use high frequencies... finely tuned and focused sound beams, intense salvos of bouncing clicks, a thousand a second, with which a hair, as thin as half a millimeter, can be detected; penetrating probes, with which they can scan the content of a colleague's stomach, follow the flow of their blood, take the full measure of an approaching brain."

It sure sounds like the description of a modern day ultrasound machine to me!

Whales can also dive to astounding depths. Another quote from Whale Nation says it beautifully.

"Curving their bodies, they dive a mile down. Dropping their heartbeat, collapsing their lungs, folding in their ribs along articulated joints to counteract the bends, happily slipping through the pressure of five hundred atmospheres, a quarter of a million tons of dense water at the seabed exerted on their bodies. Half an hour, an hour later, they emerge, triumphantly blowing like blast furnaces. Three thousand times the content of the human lung is expelled in two seconds through their air pipes in a great sigh of steam."

What would happen in a diving contest between high tech and the Highest Tech? In order to fairly evaluate this contest, there needs to be full disclosure of one of man's great ocean accomplishments. I will provide details...

although I do not consider the accomplishment a legitimate contender in the diving competition!

On January 23, 1960, the ‘Bathyscaphe Trieste’, made its historic dive. The vessel, manned by two men, descended 35,813 ft. into the Mariana Trench.

The small round sphere (which is located under the larger contraption) had walls made with special high-strength steel, five inches thick. Steel so thick it would sink the sphere like a rock, unable to resurface.

The Bathyscaphe Trieste was outfitted with a series of gasoline filled floats and nine tons of iron pellets to act as counterweights. Gasoline can withstand greater pressure than water and is lighter. The pellets are held and ready to dump when ready to return the sphere to the surface. The large contraption on top of the sphere is where the gasoline and pellets are held in order for the Trieste to resurface. It carefully descended for five hours, but only stayed down for twenty minutes due to a cracked viewing window. The return ascent took another three hours.

There was no submersible sent down again (that deep) until 2012. It was a 3-man submersible that required a large support ship to bring it to the desired location. Remember that the larger the air bubble, i.e. size of the vessel, the greater the challenge to defend it from the crushing pressures on the hull - reason for the five-inch thick walls on the small sphere.

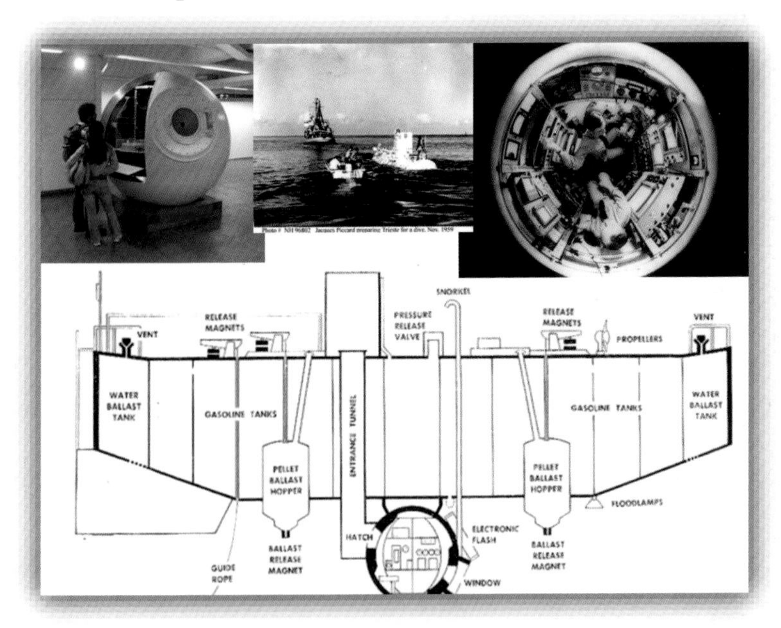

As we continue the competition, we also need to note the diving depths of two of man's military submarines.

1. The deepest diving sub: the Soviet K 278 Komsomolets (Titanium Hull) – 4,265 ft.
2. Best American Sub: "Seawolf Class" (High Grade HY-1000 Steel Hull) – 2,400 ft.

Now let's look at what God has made…

There are 3 contenders to mention. The blue whale dives to almost 700 ft. (no small feat!) and is able to stay down for 1½ hours. That's a long time to hold your breath!

But he is not the best on God's team. Next up is the Sperm whale that dives effortlessly to 7,382 feet. That is a fantastic dive – almost twice the depth of man's deepest diving submarine, not including novelty submersibles that require ships, support crew and extra equipment to resurface. Our final contestant is the Culver's Beaked Whale, diving to a depth of 9,816 ft. **with no support vessels, no gasoline tanks, no iron pellets or special assistance**! That's almost 2 miles down and would crush most submarines like a piece of tinfoil.

Remember all the extra equipment and support needed to get one small iron ball off the ocean floor and man marks this accomplishment with much fanfare. But man refuses to acknowledge and honor God for His amazing design in the whale and other creatures. So I give the Highest Tech Diving Award to God, not man!

And yes – there are other creatures "way down there" that get along just fine because God designed them to live at that crushing depth. There are shrimp and some fish that resemble flounder and sole.

Remember at 7-miles down there is pressure, darkness, cold and a limited food supply. How could these creatures evolve? Why would such creatures evolve? What would they evolve from? These are highly developed, specially designed and equipped animals that thrive in this harsh environment, because they were designed for this environment. Again, I am awestruck by the Highest Tech design!

Bacteria

We looked at something really big that God made; the whale!

Now we will look at something really, really small. Something microscopic… Bacteria! I want to talk to you about just one small part of this microscopic organism (animal).

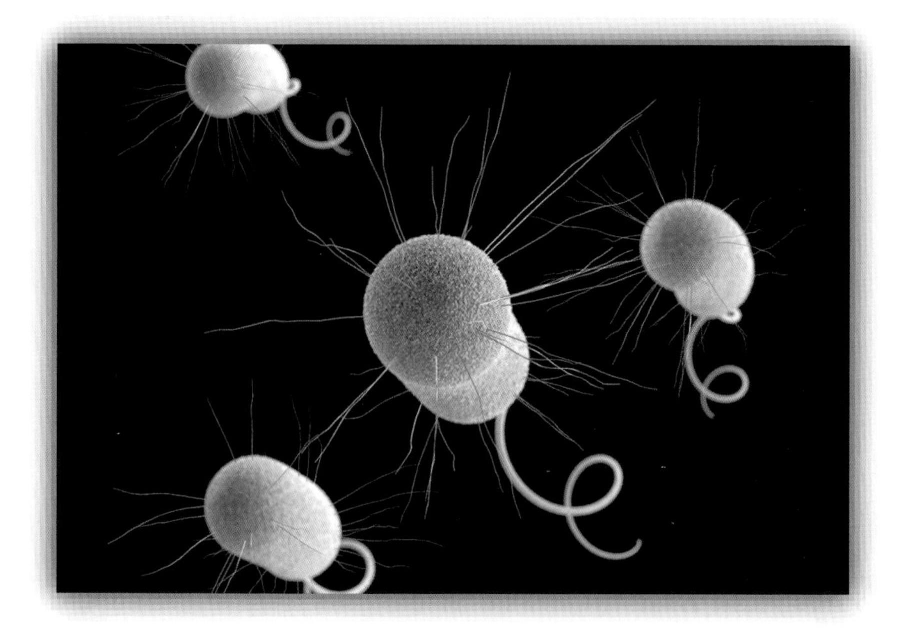

The Flagellum

The flagellum is a swimming device, the rotary propeller at the back end of a bacterium.

Note: this device differs from "cilium," in that cilium are more like "oars," to accomplish movement.

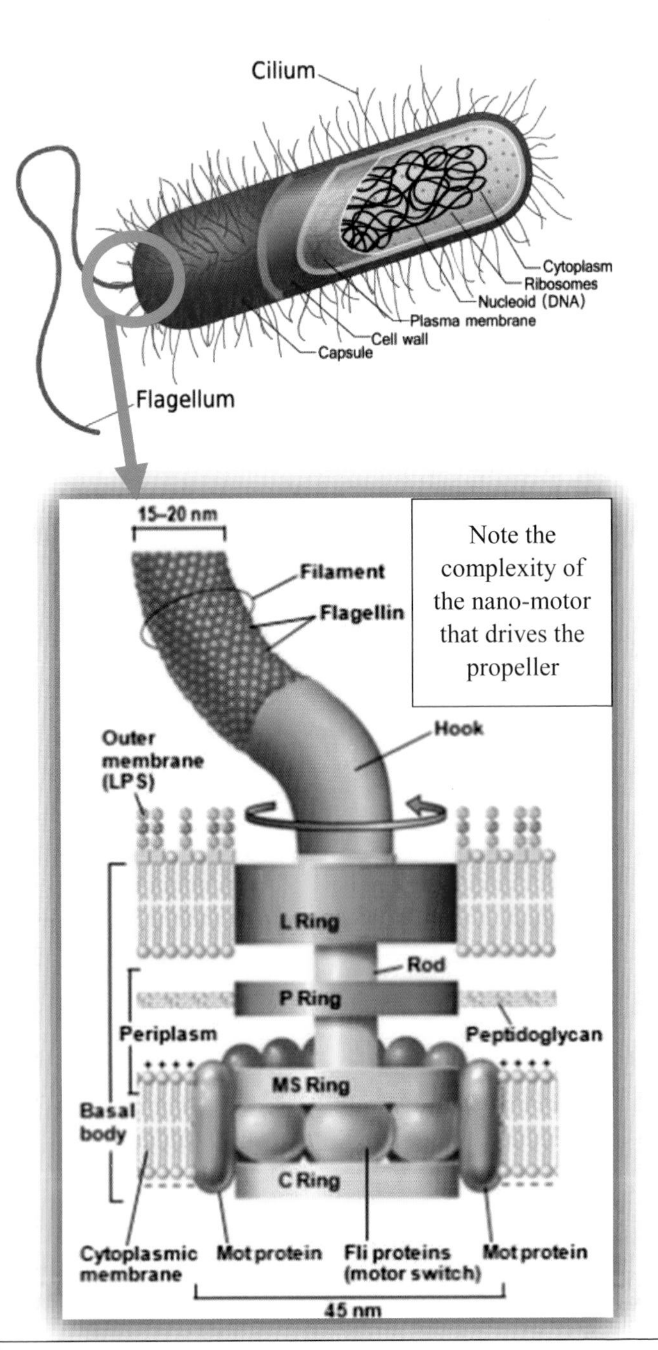

Slide by Greg Scrivin, Teacher of Physics and Science at Cranleigh School in Abu Dhabi

The flagellum is a good example of irreducible complexity! The organism needs to have this rotary propeller complete and functioning perfectly to live – period!

"No scientist has ever published a model to account for the gradual evolution of this extraordinary molecular machine." – Michael J. Behe, Professor of Biochemistry at Lehigh University

Note that the flagellum is simply the propeller and drive motor at the back end of the bacteria that enables its movement and survival.

Here are some details of this amazing propulsion system.

1. In order to produce a functioning flagellum, there are over 200 kinds of proteins needed!
2. There is a complex system where energy is generated by the flow of acid through the bacteria's membrane.
3. The rotary propeller is capable of spinning at over 100,000 RPMS.
4. The rotor can change direction in a split second. This is an insanely micro-small structure!

There is no mechanism in evolution to add new information to a DNA molecule (blueprint) in order to build the motor and propeller system in bacterium! **There is none**!

Has human technology produced any motor and/or propulsion machine that comes close to God's creation in micro-size, self-energizing, internal maintenance, 100,000 RPM performance, or the ability to stop or change direction in a millisecond? No, and yet most of secular science and society work at denying God's existence and genius. No wonder so many people are angry, confused and hopeless.

Metamorphosis

Our next example of the Highest Tech is born out of a question & answer session with post-graduate students. On one of my trips to Wichita, KS to speak at a camp for Sunrise Christian Academy, there were approximately 16 young men in the group from different countries as well as the United States. I began my hour and a half session with a simple question.

"What is your best reason to believe evolution or argument to support evolution?"

The first response was a defense of evolution, and was **exciting** because it gave me an opportunity to make several points about the religion of evolution. Here is what several in the room were "taught," is an evidence for evolution:

"The caterpillar turning into a butterfly!"

Wow! I am always amazed and sad to see how easily the promoters of evolution mislead students, and how easy it is to fool and bluff these students. By God's grace by the end of the session, three of those men prayed to receive Jesus as their Lord and Savior!

I will now make a statement and then defend it.

My statement is that metamorphosis - the transformation of a caterpillar into a butterfly, is not only a poor defense of evolution, **it is one of the most powerful modern and observable proofs of special creation!!!**

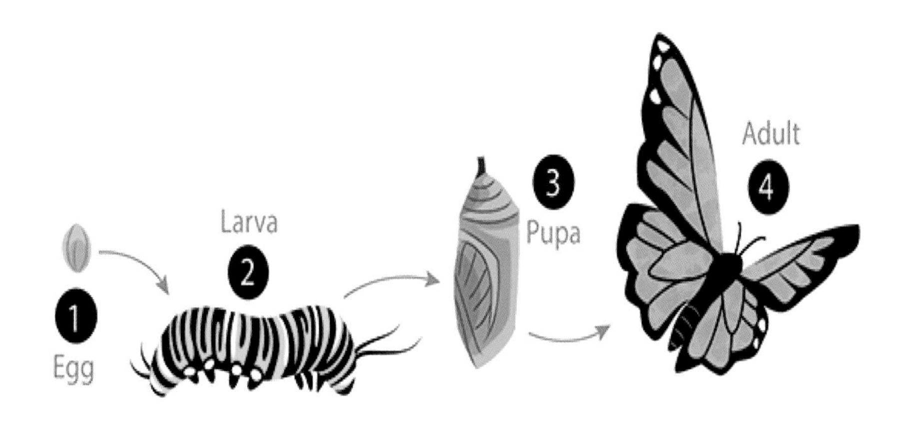

Let me tell you the fantastic story of the life cycle of a monarch butterfly.

Day one: the butterfly lays eggs on a milkweed leaf. Each of those eggs is 1.2mm in size – about the size of a strawberry seed.

A tiny caterpillar breaks out of the egg (2nd stage) and by day 9 is nearly ½ inch in length. By day 18, the caterpillar is approximately 2 inches long and going into the 3rd stage of its life cycle.

Within 8 hours of day 18, the caterpillar will use a little silk to attach itself to a branch or fixed surface and form a chrysalis.

It will shed or peel away the outer features of the caterpillar's skin and form a simple outer shell or case containing all the internal organs of the caterpillar. Now it is important to note here that in just 12 more days, on day 30 exactly, an adult butterfly is going to emerge. **On day 30, within 6 hours, a fully functional butterfly emerges.**

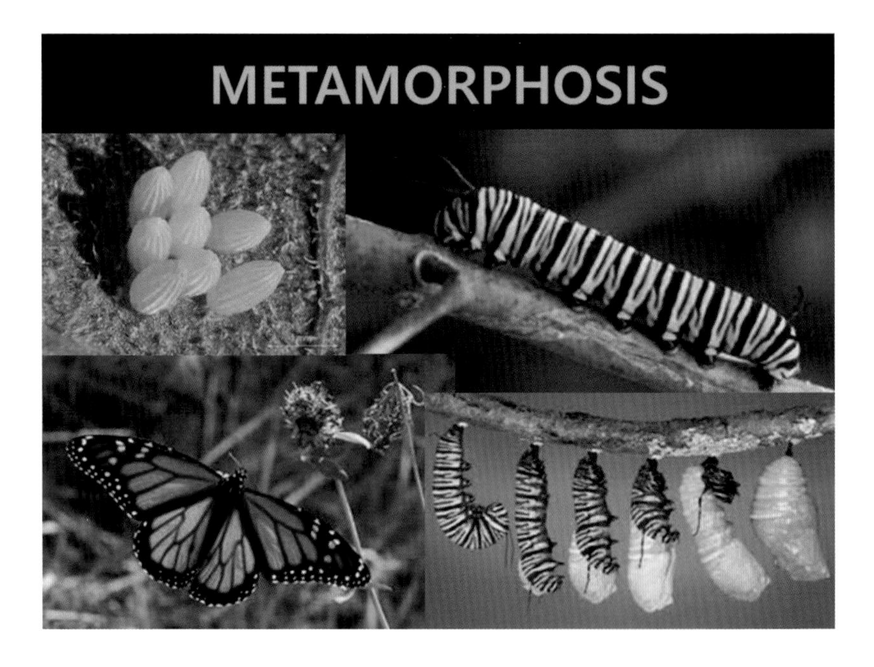

Let's review what is happening… because this is not only proof of special creation, I believe this is God demonstrating His powerful, awesome ability. Metamorphosis is a process involving four different life stages within the reproductive process to create one lifeform – the butterfly! We cannot understate this incredible design process - this reproduction is almost like magic! If we could not see and watch it happen before our eyes, no one would believe it.

Why?

You must understand what is taking place! Evolution is the teaching that over millions of years and mutations one organism is slowly transformed into a whole new creature, **BUT there is no proof that it has ever happened!**

In metamorphosis, God demonstrates that He is able, not only to produce a new animal, but He is able to do it in days, **NOT** millions of years.

And not by mutations or small successive changes, but quickly and perfectly and by supernatural means. Yes, supernatural! (This is why 3 young men prayed to receive Jesus after my session. They understood the marvel of this **complete transformation**!)

Once you fully understand and appreciate what is happening here, you will understand (if you are honest). There is no natural explanation…none. Every butterfly is a supernatural miracle!

The egg (the size of a strawberry seed) must contain the blueprints (DNA) for 3 distinct life forms: caterpillar, chrysalis, and butterfly. It must also have enough of the right protein to build what the DNA is dictating. And through it all there must be a very accurate clock, a time keeping mechanism that makes every stage and step predictable to the hour. **This is so fantastic!** Also, because there will be no parent available, all the distinct behaviors of the butterfly - what to eat, how to survive, when and where to migrate - must also be passed through the caterpillar and chrysalis stages to the adult!

Note: There is no mechanism to add additional materials or information to the caterpillar or chrysalis. All that is used to form a butterfly must be repurposed from what used to be a caterpillar. Also note that an egg the size of a strawberry seed is full mostly of protein to form the caterpillar. There is a tiny, invisible nucleus that contains **all info packets and timing equipment** for this transformation.

Consider how drastically different each life form is in appearance, function, and behavior!

Egg: Size of strawberry seed (1.2mm).

Day 1: Caterpillar (larva) sixteen stubby legs, tiny eyes, and chews leaves. Particular jaws and digestive system for roughage.

Day 18: Chrysalis (pupa) makes silk to attach itself. Sheds outer skin, color match to surroundings, organs melted into a cellular soup to reorganize.

Day 30: Butterfly (adult) now 6 long thin legs, complex compound eyes, dermal scales & color patterns, sipping straw to drink nectar, new digestive system and wings to fly.

God takes an example of the slowest moving, earthbound, blob-like creature and transforms it into a **flying, delicate, beautiful creature.** (Picture of a new birth). To somehow illustrate what man would have to pull off, in the natural world to remotely compare to what God accomplished here is truly stunning.

Day 1: Drive a school bus to the center of a parking lot.

From day 1 to day 18: Check all the fluids, wash the bus, tune it up, make sure it is in tip-top condition and ready to roll.

Day 18: Now wrap it in shrink wrap, seal it up so that nothing can be added or left over, everything inside (like the chrysalis) **must be used and nothing wasted!**

Now if we were properly matching what God does - that would be it! No more help or involvement - the bus would magically transform into an Apache attack helicopter, 12 days later. But, to give man a fighting chance to compete with God, instead of shrink wrap on the 18th day - Let's do this:

Locate the best auto, truck, and aviation repair facilities available. Assemble a team of fifty of the best mechanics, engineers, and fabricators on earth. Put the school bus in the shop. God transforms the caterpillar in 12 days. I will give the 50 man team 12 months. But there are a couple of basic rules. Although you can use all the best tools man has come up with to make things and use the smartest and most skilled people available, you must not add any new parts or equipment to the project itself, and nothing can be left over. You must repurpose everything, just as God does.

God actually breaks down all the organs of the caterpillar into their fundamental cells and proteins; then He reorganizes them into new complex organs and cell chains to produce a flying, nectar sipping, nimble, compound-eyed creature. You and your team have one year (the Lord only used 12 days and He could have done it in less!) to transform the entire bus, big truck tires, bus engine, forty seats etc. into a AH-64 Apache helicopter…that has all its armaments—fully functional night vision and radar system, runs on different fuel, speeds over 200 mph ready to fly a combat mission. Remember fully functional…

"To whom will you compare Me? Or who is My equal? says the Holy One." -Isaiah 40:25 NIV

Three Special Animals

There are an additional three animals that showcase some special and unique abilities that prompted me to include them in this book on God's Highest Tech designs.

To maximize the impact of seeing what I believe are examples of Intelligent Design in these 3 animals, I would strongly urge you to take the time to view them on YouTube or other video sources. God's design, special creation and extreme complexity in nature is amazing!

Recall my statement that evolution demands that animals should be more similar than different, with slight and cumulative changes - not the "shock and awe" of unique creatures that at times appear to be alien life forms. There are creatures that seem to be from a different planet (as in the case of Cuttlefish), or possess such a spectacular level of mathematical and geometric skills as to rival an artistic genius (as with the Japanese Puffer Fish).

The deep-sea anglers, for their part, are a group of fish that have been created with such outrageous design and behavior, and have overcome the difficulties of the environment they live in that they too deserve an honorable mention in this book. I believe, as with the other animals we have looked at, these last three demonstrate the complete failure of evolution to explain the vast array of living things that God has filled our world with.

"For since the creation of the world God's invisible qualities - His eternal power and divine nature - have been clearly seen, being understood from what has been made, so that men are without excuse."
-Romans 1:20 NIV

The Cuttlefish

The cuttlefish is neither a fish nor cuddly. It is a member of the cephalopods, which includes octopuses and squid.

One of the truly unique and specialized features this creature possesses includes the sharpest, most polarized vision in the animal kingdom, enabling them to identify even the most perfectly camouflaged prey. Cuttlefish are fierce and aggressive hunters able to overpower prey much larger than themselves.

But their real claim to fame and reason to be included in this book is their completely outrageous, unequaled and utterly fantastic camouflage system!

The cuttlefish has specially designed groups of tiny little cells in their skin called chromatophores, 200 of these special pigment cells per square millimeter. This system includes finely tuned muscles that expand and contract to create vast color combinations. This special muscle is also used to change the skin's texture. Yes, it can even mimic the basic feel and general appearance of different surroundings.

Cuttlefish Camo

I believe that God, with this one animal, tops the list of the world's greatest illusionists and magicians combined... using no props, special devices or equipment - only what God has designed into the animal biologically!

Multiple researchers of the animal have said that:

*Its color changing capability is unmatched in nature.
*There is nothing in the animal kingdom that can change its appearance as fast and as dramatically.

The cuttlefish is able to produce, match or mimic any color, including neon and strobe-like color light shows. You have to see it to believe it! That is why I recommend going to YouTube.

In addition to camouflage, the cuttlefish also uses this fantastic ability to send warnings, communicate and even hypnotize its prey!

> Note: a little extra technical info for the more "scientifically minded" concerning this color changing skin... here is how it is designed: yellow, red, black and brown chromatophores are layered above reflective white and iridescent cells to create every color, pattern and effect imaginable.

Could man with all his intellectual and technical accomplishments create a robe or cape that could match the performance of the cuttlefish's skin? No!

Japanese Puffer Fish

For my next example of God doing something so fantastic, so unexpected and mind boggling, I'd like to turn your attention to the Japanese Puffer fish.

The Japanese Puffer fish is surely one of the best (if not THE best) examples of the special and unexplainable behaviors God is able to program into the animals He designs and makes.

The little puffer is an amazing landscape artist! Quoting from a wonderful video on YouTube called Puffer Fish Creates This Blue Water Art, the narrator says the following, *"With a design of mathematical precision in his head and only fins for tools, he starts to plow the sand. He*

is sculpting it into geometric shapes. This dedicated artist works 24 hours a day for an entire week. If he stops to rest, the currents will destroy his creation."

He decorates various cross sections with shells to enhance the "wow" effect and then at last it is complete! Using only what is available on the sea bed, this little five inch fish has sculpted a masterpiece that is six feet across. And all this to attract a girlfriend! If she likes his work, he must make one last alteration.

By the next morning, he will flatten the center of the sculpture. He will make sure that all the softest sand is in the middle. He has created the perfect nest for the female to lay her eggs. When she arrives, they dance a bit, cheek to cheek. Then she releases her eggs and he fertilizes them. A quick

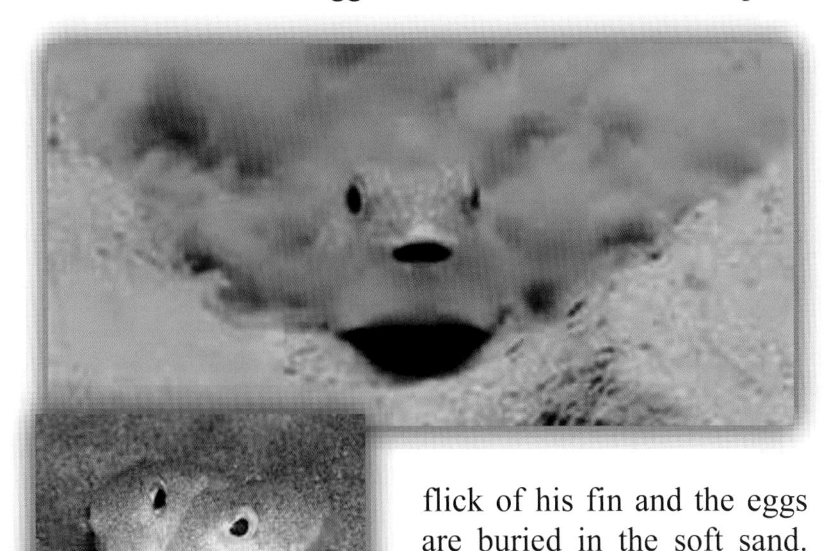

flick of his fin and the eggs are buried in the soft sand. Then she departs.

Let man (in a scuba suit) using only his hands - no tools, sculpt a similar design with perfectly symmetrical (round) portions and evenly placed geometric patterns and of course **do it to scale**. Since God's five inch artist, created a six foot masterpiece with only his fins, then I would expect that a six foot man with two strong arms and hands can sculpt (a proportional) eighty-six foot in diameter sculpture! He has a week to do it, 24 hours a day…just like God's little artist.

Yes, God made a little five-inch fish and put, "In his head a plan of geometric and mathematical perfection." Quote from BBC's Nature's Greatest Artist.

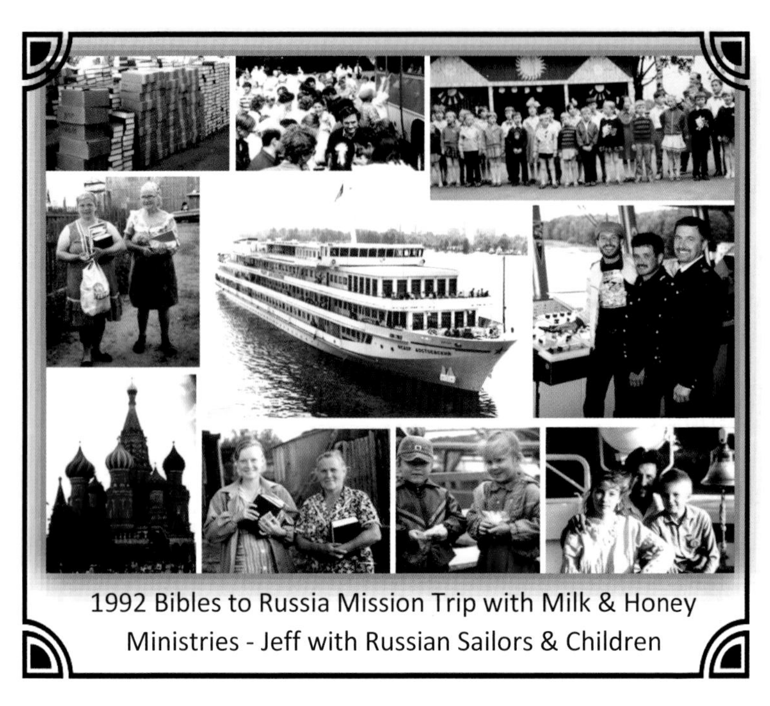

1992 Bibles to Russia Mission Trip with Milk & Honey Ministries - Jeff with Russian Sailors & Children

Deep-Sea Anglerfish

As we come to our last creature, she is certainly a favorite with young people when I give one of my nature talks. Not to mention, she is also a favorite "Awe Moment" of my good and longtime friend and mentor, Dr. Rob Lindsted. **Brother Rob, this one is for you!**

Due to the dark, cold, deep depths where these creatures live, they have only been filmed in their natural environment less than a half-dozen times. It is rare indeed to see these mysterious fish in their undeniably harsh and challenging environment.

But again God does the unexpected - creating and equipping a unique creature to live in this specific environment. **Evolutionists have not and cannot explain any of the wonder that I am about to share with you.**

This animal would never evolve and would certainly not choose to live at the depth it lives.

An aquatic researcher from a YouTube clip, Deep Sea Anglers, said the following, *"The deep is full of surprises and wonderful creatures. Humans have only just begun to explore this vast realm and we can only imagine what discoveries are yet to be made."*

The deep-sea angler fish makes its home hundreds of feet below the ocean's surface where it is dark and cold. (The sun rays are absorbed closer to the surface). At depths of 650 feet and below—the environment is a very harsh, freezing temperature, almost total darkness, and under tremendous water pressure (which increases 15 lbs. per square inch for every 33 feet of depth).

All these factors make food scarce and hard to locate and catch. But God, has given the deep-sea angler some very special equipment.

So what equipment do you need to catch food in water when it is dark? How about a fishing pole & flashlight?

This fish has a built-in, movable fishing pole mounted to its head above the mouth. It also has the ability to light up the phony bait/lure at the tip. The angler can remain motionless and without seeing; feeling with special sensory organs in its skin the slightest movement around her.

As the prey comes near, it is enticed with the wiggling of the lure in front of her huge mouth. Then at just the right moment, she opens her mouth in a split-second causing a powerful suction while lunging forward...dinner is served!

By the way, "the flashlight" is able to light up the lure through the use of bioluminescence. (This is not fully understood by scientists). The angler has an expandable stomach, in case it gets lucky with a really big meal. Also, to ensure that there is no chance of the prey escaping, there are teeth in its throat.

There is one more important part of the Angler's life that is also challenging and unique. It's very difficult to find a mate in these dark harsh conditions. God decided to solve the problem with a behavior so bizarre that the evolutionists would go crazy trying to explain it.

First, the female angler is much larger than the male angler. I mean he is really a little dude. And the way this behavior works, is that when a male finds a female, he literally sinks his teeth into her and hangs on and on, for the rest of his life. In one certain species of Angler, the male becomes a life-long parasite. The skin around his mouth and jaws fuse with the female's body.

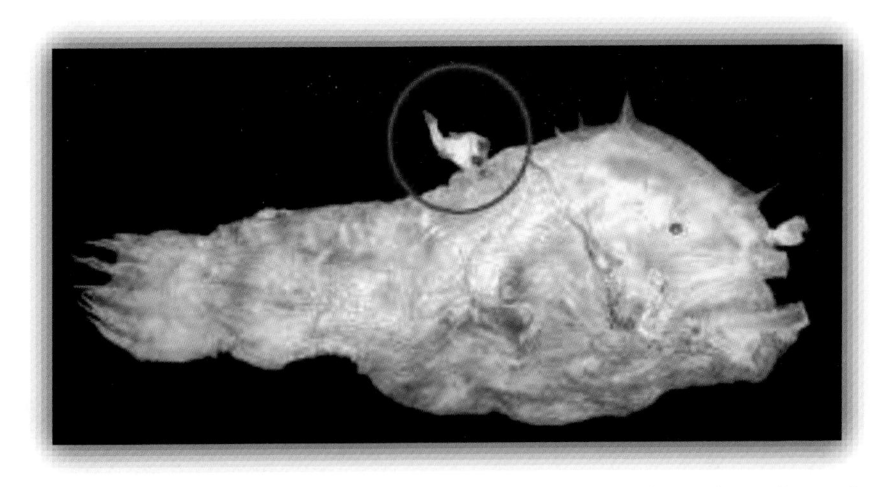

In order to have a more accurate and detailed explanation of this bizarre mating behavior, I am including a quote from the book, Secrets of the Sea – Life in the Depths, page 113.

"Certain deep-dwelling anglers possess adaptations for reproduction as astonishing as those for feeding. In the dark, sparsely populated depths, these fishes may have difficulty finding a mate. Therefore, when a male meets a female, he sinks his teeth into her and hangs on – sometimes for the rest of his life. If he belongs to the species whose males are lifelong parasites, the skin around his mouth and jaws fuses with the female's body; only a small opening for breathing remains on either side of his mouth. His eyes degenerate as do most of his internal organs. His circulatory system becomes connected with hers, and from then on he is nourished by her blood. In effect, the male becomes an external appendage producing sperm to fertilize the female's eggs.

Although the female probably releases her eggs in the deep sea, they quickly float upward and hatch in surface waters, where the newborn find plenty of copepods and other small plankton to eat. As they grow, females begin to develop fishing poles and males acquire gripping teeth on their snouts and chins. When the anglers change from larvae to adults, they descend to deep water and take up their strange way of life."

The lifestyle (especially the reproductive process) of this fish is so outrageous and complex; it screams of special design! There is nothing in nature similar in form or function that this fish could have evolved from… NOTHING!

Jeff in Wichita, Kansas, S.E.W. Camp with Sunrise Christian Academy, Community Bible Chapel with Mike & Carole, with Pam & Zama (who minister in Burma) and with Ron

D.N.A. Deoxyribonucleic Acid

(God's Blueprint for Every Living Thing)

DNA is the most compact information transporting system in the universe! Most important, DNA is a language, and every language has an author. Jesus is the author of LIFE!

"For You created my inmost being; You knit me together in my mother's womb. I praise You because I am fearfully and wonderfully made; Your works are wonderful, I know that full well."
-Psalm 139:13-14 NIV

In every human being there are 30 trillion cells. In each cell, there are 46 chromosomes (23 from mom and 23 from dad) all coiled up together like tiny springs. If uncoiled and stretched out, end-to-end they would measure 7 feet long, but would be so thin that you could not see the strand, even with an Electron Microscope. This strand of 46 Chromosomes is in a Double Helix form, and is called DNA. It is all coded information - the information to make each of us. Every cell has a duplicate copy.

The written equivalent from just one cell would fill a large library of 4,000 books. **That's the information in just one cell!** The total amount of coded information in the human body is mind boggling! The DNA strand from every cell in the body (30 trillion cells) placed end to end would go from here to the moon 100,000 times, and yet the genetic material would not even fill two teaspoons!

Look at it another way. If we converted all the information from all 30 trillion cells to its written equivalent, how many books do you think that would fill? The book equivalent would fill the Grand Canyon over 40 times!!

But wait, I'm not sure you know how big of an area that is. The Grand Canyon is one mile deep, several miles wide in places, but most importantly it extends more than 200 miles. The information contained in just one human being, converted to books would fill that space OVER 40 TIMES!

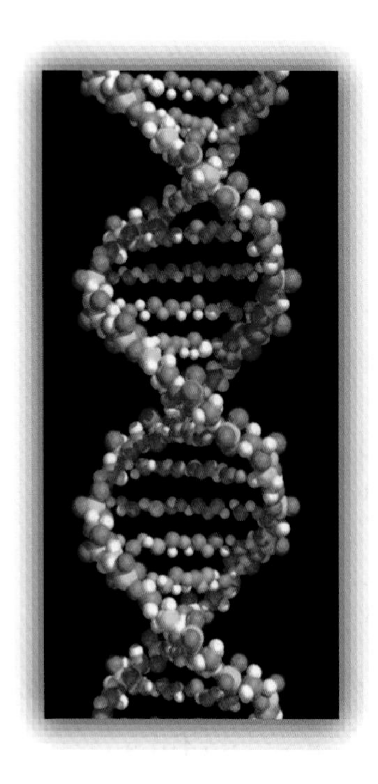

Now, please go back and reread Psalm 139:13-14. ***"...we are fearfully and wonderfully made..."*** Dr. Francis Crick, the co-discoverer of the DNA molecule said that "the DNA molecule is so complex that the probability of it forming by itself is **ZERO – IMPOSSIBLE!"**

Now let's compare this to man's information storage devices. The DNA material that would fill just 20% of a teaspoon would require **one trillion** (1 with 12 zeros) compact disks (cd's) to hold the same amount of information.

Our God Is Without Limits! It is mind-boggling to consider God's power and design in nature! His ability is to make things really big and really small and everything in between. Could God have made the universe larger? Yes! But we can't reach the limits of the universe He has made. It took a long time for man to invent the telescope and space exploration devices. Could God have made things smaller and more complex? Again the answer is yes! God is without limits. But we have limitations in our own equipment. He wants us to be able to discover and see the awesome nano-structures He has created in nature and all living things.

Would you - by yourself - with no other biased influence, conclude that looking at anything clearly designed with purpose: a chair, car, toaster, tea cup, bicycle, toilet paper, etc. is the result of chaos and time or random luck?

Jeff & Team in Quito, Ecuador 2001
Building and Medical Mission Trip

Above: Jeff on a Medical & Evangelism Trip to Romania in 1994. The team visited mountain villages and orphanages.

Below: Jeff's next Trip to Romania in 1998
The team took in humanitarian aid for orphans.

The "Time" Argument

I need to address one more issue before resting my case in defense of special creation by an all-powerful Creator God. I read many science papers, research articles and books written by believers in evolution. I have discovered a common and often repeated belief that has become an almost universal response answer to anyone asking a question involving the great **COMPLEXITY** and **DESIGN** in nature.

That response stated in slightly different ways simply says, "Enough TIME is the answer…"

"Evolution can do amazing things given enough TIME."
-Associated Press Article

This quote clearly represents what has become the most common response by evolutionists to all the difficult questions and challenges to their (religious) belief. The idea that NO designer, NO creator, NO source of chemistry, NO source of life, NO source of information PLUS time (lots of time) will give us the **incredible variety of complex life forms** we see on earth!!!

BIG PROBLEM: Time is in reality (a scientific fact) the enemy of the evolutionary theory. One of the most basic and fundamental Laws of Physics is the 2nd Law of Thermodynamics which produces the OPPOSITE of what evolution requires in order to have a hope.

Need proof? It is time to be honest about your experiences with the world in which we live.

EVERYTHING, when subjected to time, degrades, breaks down, becomes more random – not the reverse! Food, clothes, cars, metal, wood, paint, homes, appliances are all getting old and fading, rusting, rotting, crumbling, dying, etc.!

Common sense and life experience clearly teach us and demonstrate this obvious truth! But the desire to reject a loving, all powerful Creator God is so strong that otherwise smart people are willing to cast reality to the side in order to embrace a belief that does not acknowledge God.

Evolution Requires Faith! Another example of this faith in the "magic of time" is the often cited illustration of… 1,000,000 monkeys typing on 1,000,000 typewriters for 1,000,000 years and (based on probability) saying one of them might actually type a coherent page of information! **No, they would not!** In the real world, you would have 1,000,000 broken typewriters.☺

The **TRUTH** is:

1. God's creative works are endless!
2. NO ONE can fully explain the intricate and complex designs of God in creation!
3. God's glory surrounds our lives and many choose to ignore, or worse – deny it BELONGS to HIM!
4. *"He performs wonders that cannot be fathomed, miracles that cannot be counted"* -Job 5:9 NIV

It is important to understand that no life-forms (animals, plants or people) are exempt from the 2nd Law of Thermodynamics. This is not difficult to see and prove. From the time of birth, or plants springing up from the ground; all things immediately begin to age and will according to their designed life expectancy, die. Nothing organic escapes this law and evolution is no exception.

Life systems are not evolving into other and/or better life forms. They are not becoming more complex. Life systems are wearing out, becoming weaker (after passing through the prime years of their life cycle) and will ultimately die and wither away. LIFE now and ETERNAL life, only come through the Life-Giver, our Lord and Savior Jesus Christ!

> In John 11:25-26 NIV, Jesus said, ***"I am the Resurrection and the Life. He who believes in Me will live, even though he dies; and whosoever lives and believes in Me will never die. Do you believe this?"***

A note from the author…

Thank you for taking the time to read this book. I pray that you would understand the clear implication of God's incredible design in nature. Pause for a moment and consider the tremendous effort and complexity God has woven into nature in order to capture the attention of the youngest child and the most accomplished scientist. Jesus is constantly, lovingly, seeking to get our attention, so that we would receive His message of love, and understand our need for salvation. Once He has our attention, we must respond to His plan for salvation.

Two common attitudes that keep people from salvation are:

1. I'm okay, I'm not that bad, God will accept me as I am.
2. God will not send a "basically good" person to hell - the old argument that a loving and merciful God will not send sincere, well-meaning sinners to hell.

My friend, if you could live a life worthy of heaven (perfect), then Christ would have died for nothing. No person can be forgiven apart from Jesus Christ!

> ***"As it is written: There is no one righteous, not even one; there is no one who understands; no one who seeks God. All have turned away, they have together become worthless; there is no one who does good, not even one."***
>
> ***"Therefore no one will be declared righteous in God's sight by the works of the law; rather, through the law we become conscious of our sin."***
>
> ***-Romans 3:10-12, 20 NIV***

For it is by grace you have been saved, through faith—and this is not from yourselves, it is the gift of God - not by works, so that no one can boast.
-Ephesians 2:8-9 NIV

If you believe that the love and mercy of God will insulate you from the penalty of hell, consider this, "Where was the love and mercy of God when His only Son was being brutally crucified?"

This question is difficult to answer because you do not comprehend the seriousness of your sin, and the unfathomable depth of God's love. In order to remain righteous - God must judge sin! In order for God to demonstrate His love, He must act! And act He did! God's solution was a substitutionary death. In other words, He paid our sin debt Himself. That is why trusting in Jesus is not optional, it is the only solution to our dilemma.

Expecting to enter heaven, without trusting that Jesus died on the cross in our place is like saying, "I believe Jesus died on the cross, but He did not have to die for me. I'm okay, I'm not that bad, God knows me..." Yes, God knows we are self-deluded, prideful sinners that are more interested in doing things our way than submitting to His Word. God tells us that we must accept Jesus as our Lord and Savior!

Salvation is as simple as ABC:

Agree with God that we are hell deserving sinners and turn from sin.

Believe that only trusting in the finished work of Jesus and asking Him to be your Savior is the answer.

Confess your decision for Christ with others as you live for Him and Praise His Name!

You have the God-given freedom to think and believe whatever you choose, but remember all our choices have consequences! So before you make a choice concerning something so important – at least take the time to consider, just a little of the evidence for creation. The wonder of "Intelligent Design" has successfully been blocked from entering many of the classrooms in America, where only ideas that support the accepted or official theory are allowed. I hope I have remedied that in this book and you now realize how much God loves His creation and how much He loves you!

Jeff's favorite verses for
"The Highest Tech"

Psalm 104:24 NLT- "O Lord, what a variety of things you have made! In wisdom you made them all. The Earth is full of your creatures."

Psalm 33:8 KJV- "Let all the earth fear the LORD: Let all the inhabitants of the world stand in awe of Him."

Job 12:7-10 NIV- "But ask the animals, and they will teach you, or the birds of the air, and they will tell you; or speak to the earth, and it will teach you, or let the fish of the sea inform you. Which of all these does not know that the hand of the Lord has done this? In His hand is the life of every creature and the breath of all mankind."

In Conclusion

A quote by Michael Kelly, in an article entitled EVOLUTION – AN ARTICLE OF FAITH, states it well, ***"Charles Darwin admitted that the available fossil evidence didn't support his theory of 'survival of the fittest,' better known as evolution. But he expected that plenty of evidence would be found in coming years. Now, more than a century and a half later, the evidence still fails to support his theory – showing people accept Darwinian evolution more as an article of faith rather than of fact."***

PLEASE CONSIDER the following admission by a professor who is an authority on the life and beliefs of Charles Darwin.

Michael Ruse, professor of history and philosophy and author of THE DARWINIAN REVOLUTION (1979), and TAKING DARWIN SERIOUSLY (1986), acknowledges that evolution is religious: ***"Evolution is promoted by its practitioners as more than mere science. Evolution is promulgated as an ideology, a secular religion - a full-fledged alternative to Christianity, with meaning and morality. I am an ardent evolutionist and an ex-Christian, but I must admit in this one complaint... the literalists (i.e. creationists) are absolutely right. Evolution is a religion. This was true of evolution in the beginning, and it is true of evolution still today."***

Note: In order to qualify as a scientific fact, a theory must be observable or reproducible. Creation and evolution fail on both accounts, therefore both theories are a matter of faith! The question is... what scientific discoveries best support your theory and ultimate faith?!

I hope I showed you through nature evidence for an Intelligent Designer – the Lord Jesus!